Sticks & Stones

Words That Build, Not Break

Craig A. Smith

Sticks & Stones: Words That Build, Not Break

© Craig A. Smith, 2024

All rights reserved. Except as may be permitted by the Copyright Act, no part of this publication may be reproduced in any form or by any means without prior permission from the publisher.

Unless otherwise noted, Scripture quotations are taken from THE HOLY BIBLE, NEW INTERNATIONAL VERSION®, NIV® copyright © 1973, 1978, 1984, 2011 by Biblica, Inc. ™

Used by permission. All rights reserved worldwide.

Contents

1 - The Power of Words 5
2 - Words in the Modern World 15
3 - The Most ~~Dangerous~~ Powerful Part of Your Body ... 25
    The Bad News 26
    The Good News 29
4 - Primum Non Nocere 33
5 - Is It True? 45
    What is truth? 48
    Can we know truth? 51
    Echo Chambers 58
    Breaking Out of Our Echo Chambers 63
6 - Tasty Truth 65
    Truth and Kindness 71
7 - Is It Kind? 77
    The 4 C's of Kindness 82
8 – The Four Worlds 85
    Flattery 86
    Gossip 88
    Slander 95
    Grace 98
9 - In These Last Days 99

10- Which Spirit Is Speaking? 107

11 - The Final Word 123

Why Write This Book?

In writing this short book, I have hoped to do three fairly simple, yet critically important, things.

First, I have hoped to impress upon you, my reader, the power of your words. Like the sticks and stones to which sometimes contrast them, words can build or they can break. Words create worlds, but they also tear them down. I think the first step to using words wisely is understanding exactly why we *must* use them wisely, why we cannot afford to wield them as though they had no weight, no heft, no substance.

We live in a world of words. We call this the Information Age, but in practical terms, this means we live in the Age of Words. There have never been so many words, produced so easily, distributed so effortlessly, impacting so broadly. Unfortunately, the ease with which all these words can be "spoken" can leave us with the impression that there's not much to them.

Nothing could be further from the truth.

Second, I have hoped to make it clear that how we talk to and about other people tells other people a lot about us. And even more importantly, as Christians, how we talk to and about other people tells other people a lot about the Jesus we claim to follow. As followers of Jesus, we cannot afford to use our words in ways that give others a distorted perception of our Savior, especially if we have any hope that he will become their Savior as well.

I am increasingly concerned that the way Christians in the United States of America are talking to and about those we disagree with is at odds with the instruction God gave us through the Apostle Peter:

> **But in your hearts revere Christ as Lord. Always be prepared to give an answer to everyone who asks you to give the reason for the hope that you have. But do this with gentleness and respect, keeping a clear conscience, so that those who speak maliciously against your good behavior in Christ may be ashamed of their slander.**
>
> *- 1 Peter 3:15-16*

I understand the concerns, fears, and frustrations of many Christians which prompt the kind of speeches, sermons, posts, and comments I'm talking about. I not only *understand* the concerns, but in the vast majority of cases, I *share* them. What I do not share is the belief that these concerns justify speaking in ways that Jesus did not model and, in fact, explicitly forbade.

I saw a post recently in which someone said, "Dear Christians, it's not just that I don't believe in Jesus, it's that I don't think YOU believe in Jesus!" The post then went on to describe several interactions with people who claimed to follow Jesus but spoke to and about other people in ways that, at least to this individual, couldn't be reconciled with the Jesus he had read about in the Bible.

I wish I could say I read this post and thought "oh, you're making that up", but truth be told, what I thought was, "I know exactly what you're talking about."

There's a song called *Explaining Jesus* by Jordy Searcy. It's buried pretty deep in my Spotify "liked" list. It doesn't come up very often but recently I was on a very long walk and had time to revisit some old songs I tagged years ago. I heard this song again and discovered that some if its lyrics mirror my own motivation in writing this book:

> *I'm so sorry*
> *For what you've heard*
> *We're broken poets*
> *With silly words*
> *We paint agendas*
> *And call it truth*
> *I'm sorry no one explained Jesus to you*

I don't know if Searcy and I are on exactly the same page about everything theologically, but on this at least, we couldn't be closer: I'm tired of having to say to people who don't know Jesus, "I'm sorry for how you've been spoken to by those who claim to follow Jesus."

Third, I have hoped to equip you, in some practical ways, to use your words a little more wisely. To use them to build up rather than to break down. If our sticks and stones are going to be used to break anything, it should be the walls of hostility, conflict, misunderstanding, and apathy.

4

1 - The Power of Words

Some of the things we learn as kids turn out to be really useful when we grow up.

"Treat others as you want to be treated" and "honesty is the best policy" are pretty good principles whether you're eight or eighty.

But let's be honest: not everything we learn as kids stood the test of time.

Sometimes the ideas were good starting points, but too simplistic to serve as universal guiding principles.

"Good things come to those who wait" springs to mind. Is patience a virtue? Yes. Does paralysis or fear sometimes disguise itself as patience and keep us from seizing good opportunities? Also, yes.

"Everything happens for a reason" feels like another good example. Does God bring good things out of bad circumstances? Absolutely. Does that mean God created the bad circumstances so He could do a good thing? Not at all.

(To be fair, I do actually think everything happens for a reason; I just think sometimes the reason is that people make really bad decisions!)

And then there are some things we were told as kids that turned out to be lies from the pit of hell itself.

Probably the best example of this is something many of us heard growing up:

Sticks and stones may break my bones, but words will never hurt me

Remember that one?

Did you believe it then?

How about now?

Apparently, this little bit of so-called wisdom goes back at least to 1872, when it appeared in an edition of *The Christian Recorder*. In its original context, it was actually a pretty useful principle. See, originally, it wasn't meant to deny that words have power but to stiffen our spines against that power when summoning the courage to do what is right, "despite the jeers and sneers of our companions" which is how the original aphorism ended.

The way most of us heard it, though, the clear implication was that words don't hurt.

And we all know that's a lie.

"You're stupid."

"You're ugly."

"You're fat."

"You're fired."

"I don't love you anymore."

"I wouldn't go out with you if you were the last man on earth."

"I want to live with dad."

"That's the dumbest idea I've ever heard."

You've probably got a few of your own, don't you?

Why would we ever tell kids that words will never hurt them when we're all walking around with the wounds they've inflicted?

It's been said that "words create worlds", and that's true, but let's be honest: they also tear them down. Words hurt. Maybe the damage can't be seen on our bodies, but it can be felt in our souls. And the damage they cause heals – if at all – far more slowly than broken bones.

Words don't even have to be spoken in anger to do deep damage.

I still remember being back from college for the summer and going to my barber. After a little bit of catching up, she got to work on what I honestly thought of as my pretty impressive head of hair. Somewhere mid-cut, she just casually threw out words that I still remember to this day, more than three decades later: "Wow, you're really starting to lose your hair, aren't you?"

Ouch. I've never considered myself particularly vain, but that really stung! And I know, she wasn't being mean or intending to cause me any pain at all but...well, here I am bringing it up again thirty years later in a book about the power of words!

Words hurt, and sometimes they keep on hurting for a long time.

I broke a finger recently and while the orthopedic surgeon was looking at the x-rays, he pointed to a jagged white line on another finger and said, "Looks like this isn't first finger you've ever broken. How'd you break that one?"

No idea.

Literally, no idea.

I assume I felt it at the time and just thought I had jammed it or sprained it or something, but I don't even remember that.

So, I've literally broken bones that I have no memory of, but things people have said to me seem to stay fresh no matter how much time passes.

Chances are you have a physical scar or two you don't remember how you got, but you've also got some word-wounds whose origin story is crystal clear even decades later.

Recent studies in epigenetics – the science of how genes are turned on or off - have discovered that words can, quite literally, change our brains by influencing the expression of genes that regulate stress.[1] Positive words can strengthen areas of the brain that promote cognitive function and stimulate motivation. But even a single negative word can increase activity in the amygdala, releasing stress hormones.

Words don't just *hurt*, they harm, and the harm they produce can be profound and long-lasting.

And, clever rhymes aside, we have always known it.

As I was researching the origin of "sticks and stones may break my bones, but words will never hurt me", I discovered that another very well-known saying about words made its first appearance just a few years earlier:

---

[1] Andrew Newberg and Mark Robert Waldman, *Words Can Change Your Brain* (Penguin Group, 2013)

The pen is mightier than the sword.

- Edward Bulwer-Lytton

That one isn't told to kids nearly as often, but it should be, because it's an important reminder about the power we wield with our words.

But our understanding that words are powerful – far more powerful than we seem to remember as we sling them about like harmless playthings – goes back much further than the 19th century.

At least as far back as ancient Greece, philosopher-poets drew our attention to the same reality:

I have often regretted my speech, but never my silence.

- Simonedes, 4th Century B.C.

Even earlier than that, perhaps as early as the 10th century B.C., the Israelite King Solomon wrote:

Sin is not ended by multiplying words, but the prudent hold their tongues.

- Proverbs 10:19

Have you ever heard the old saying, "better to stay silent and be thought a fool than to open your mouth and remove all doubt"? Turns out old King Solomon might deserve credit for that one:

Even fools are thought wise if they keep silent, and discerning if they hold their tongues.

- Proverbs 17:28

Solomon may have also penned the words:

Many words mark the speech of a fool.

- Ecclesiastes 5:3

Centuries after Solomon, the Greeks encoded their reverence for the power of words into their word for words. The Greek term for "word" is *logos*, which meant far more than just a set of letters, the sound they make, or the thing or idea the sound represents. *Logos* was universal divine reason, the mind which underlay, gave rise to, and held together, all of nature.

For the Greeks, words didn't merely *represent* the world, they *created* it.

Building on this understanding, the *Gospel of John* describes Jesus - the divine Son who has come into the world - as the *Word (logos) become flesh* (John 1:14):

In the beginning was the Word, and the Word was with God, and the Word was God.

- John 1:1

This was John's way of building on the Greek conception of *logos* to say that Jesus is not merely a word *from* God, a messenger with a message for the world, he is the Word *of* God, the personal, creative force through whom the world itself was created. Or, as John went on to say in the next verse:

> **Through him all things were made; without him nothing was made that has been made.**
>
> *- John 1:2*

The ancients understood very well that words do not simply *convey*, they *create*. Words create worlds; worlds of beauty, peace and healing, but also – as we all know far too well - worlds of horror, pain and suffering.

James, the half-brother of Jesus understood this clearly:

> **When we put bits into the mouths of horses to make them obey us, we can turn the whole animal. Or take ships as an example. Although they are so large and are driven by strong winds, they are steered by a very small rudder wherever the pilot wants to go. Likewise, the tongue is a small part of the body, but it makes great boasts. Consider what a great forest is set on fire by a small spark. The tongue also is a fire, a world of**

evil among the parts of the body. It corrupts the whole body, sets the whole course of one's life on fire, and is itself set on fire by hell.

- The Epistle of James 3:3-6

Words are powerful. We've always known it.

And yet, we often forget it, which is an amnesia we cannot afford.

2 - Words in the Modern World

Forgetting the power of words is like carrying around a sharp stick and forgetting we have it in our hands. You don't have to be trying to hurt someone to do a lot of damage.

In another biblical proverb, King Solomon warned us of precisely that inadvertent danger:

> **The words of the reckless pierce like swords.**
>
> *- Proverbs 12:18*

Reckless words have always been dangerous, but the danger is even greater in the modern world, not because words have become more powerful, but because reckless words now have a vastly greater range.

Instead of swords, our words have become guns.

Instead of having to get up close and personal to do harm, our words can now operate at a great distance.

Why does that matter?

Think about this: the overwhelming majority of murders in the U.S. are committed with guns (about 80%).[2] Conversely, only about 10% of murders are committed with blades.

Why is that?

Well of course, it's partly because guns can more easily kill multiple people at the same time. With a knife, when an attacker is stabbing someone, bystanders can overpower and disarm him. That's a lot harder to do with a gun which can be turned on not just a single individual but on a large crowd. So that's certainly part of it.

And, of course, guns can do more damage with less effort, and in a smaller amount of time.

But there's another factor we can't afford to ignore: there is a profound psychological difference between standing at a distance and shooting a projectile *at* someone, and standing next to someone and driving a blade *into* them. The *physical* distance that guns allow for create a

---

[2] See https://www.pewresearch.org/short-reads/2023/04/26/what-the-data-says-about-gun-deaths-in-the-u-s/

psychological distance, and this distance allows for a separation of the act from the consequence.

Not to be graphic, but with a knife, an attacker not only sees the effect, he feels it. He feels the body of his victim resist then give way to the blade, he feels the shudder of the victim through the blade, his own hand, his own arm, and ultimately in his own body.

But none of that's true with a gun.

Let me be clear: this isn't an anti-gun argument. I know the issue of gun control in our country is hotly contested, in part, because it's highly complicated. I have no interest in wading into that debate.

My point isn't that guns are worse than knives. My point is that one of the reasons more murders are committed with guns than knives is that guns work from a distance and this distance creates a psychological buffer between the action and the effect.

What does this have to do with words?

In the modern world, words act more like guns than knives, more like assault rifles than swords.

Words have always been powerful, but in the past, you had to get up close and personal to use them.

Yes, you could write letters...assuming you were literate which wasn't widespread until recently. And a few people could write newspaper or magazine articles. And fewer people still could write books and get them published and distributed.

But generally speaking, until quite recently, very few people had the ability to impact more than a few individuals with their words.

For most people, for most of history, the power of their words was restricted to a small sphere of influence: husband or wife, kids, parents, friends, a few close neighbors, etc.

Of course, they could do great damage inside that small sphere, but their words were very much like the blade Solomon had in mind when he said that the words of the reckless pierce like swords. Reckless words have always been dangerous, but they were dangerous only to those in their immediate vicinity.

But today, with hardly any effort whatsoever, words circle the world. Reckless words from anyone can be dangerous to everyone. Just think about how fast an X post or an Instagram reel can garner more than a hundred thousand views.

And it's not just about how easy they are to *propagate*. It's about how easy they are to *produce*.

Compare the amount of effort that used to go into writing a letter to the amount of effort required to send a text. Compare the amount of effort that used to go into writing a book and getting it published to the amount of effort required to post something on social media.

And remember that the amount of *effort* required to produce something has a direct impact on how much *thought* is put into its production. The longer it takes to produce something, the more you think about whether or not you actually *want* to produce it. And the longer it takes to produce it, the more you're thinking about what you're producing as you're producing it.

Anyone who's ever written an email or a text and then wisely chosen to wait before sending it knows how often reflection changes our perception of what we've produced.

That kind of reflection used to be built-in to the time-consuming process of so much of our communication. Writing a letter used to mean finding paper and a pen and then the laborious process of putting pen to paper and writing legible sentences. I'm confident many a nasty letter didn't get written because it was just too much work.

Then, once a letter was done, you had to get an envelope, pick up the letter again and fold it so it would fit in the envelope, seal the envelope, get a stamp, take it to the mailbox, etc. That's a lot of built-in time for reflection on the question of whether or not you really should send those words out into the world.

But none of that's true anymore.

Never have so many words been sent out into the world with so little effort...and therefore with so little reflection on their impact on the world.

We should also consider the fact that the gatekeepers are gone. What I mean is that sharing your words with more than a select few used to require getting certain people to agree that the words *should* be shared more widely.

Just think about the way the publishing industry has changed. It used to be if you wanted to write a book, you had to actually write a book, which was a long and rather tedious process. Now you can get an AI to do most or all of the work for you. Sure, you can still tell the difference between something a human being wrote and something an AI produced. But, the very fact that there is free access to Large Language Model AI systems that can instantly produce whole books is a mind-boggling change to our intellectual landscape. You quite seriously no longer have to write a book to write a book.

In the past, writing the book was only the first hurdle to getting your words out to the world. The next hurdle was getting someone to distribute it, and that was an even bigger barrier. Printing books was expensive, which meant that publishing companies were selective about which books they printed. They wanted to make sure the books would sell and that the contents wouldn't cause the company embarrassment. So, there were editors and fact-checkers and marketing departments who had to get involved. And then, of course, you had to convince bookstores to actually carry the book.

Similar gatekeepers existed for magazines, trade journals, and newspapers. In the past, by the time something was made available for mass consumption, it had usually been read, considered, second-guessed, tweaked, trimmed, qualified and nuanced by multiple people. It had convinced a lot of people that it was worth sharing with a lot of people.

Now, to be fair, none of this means that there wasn't a lot of garbage that got published in the past, but it was a higher-quality garbage!

Also, to be fair, the process of getting past the gate-keepers meant that a lot of things that should have been more widely propagated never were. Biases, prejudices, commercial concerns and a host of other hard-to-pin-down filters often kept important words in small circles.

I'm not saying things were necessarily better back then. I'm saying things were different and we need to understand how things have changed and be aware of what those changes mean when it comes to our own words.

We live in an age where, without the scrutiny of a single fact checker or editor conscious of the social impact, anyone can share their words with the world.

Fifty years ago, getting our thoughts out to more than a couple dozen people was extremely difficult. But today, when a social media post goes viral – and the most unexpected of them often do – the impact is not on dozens but hundreds, and often on thousands or even on millions of people around the world.

Into this present reality, Jesus' warning about words feels a lot like a much-needed wake-up call:

> **"But I tell you that everyone will have to give account on the day of judgment for every careless[3] word they have spoken. For by your words you will be acquitted, and by your words you will be condemned."**
>
> *- Matthew 12:36-37*

From the proverbs of Solmon to the preaching of Jesus, the Bible consistently warns that, not only are reckless words dangerous, they are sins for which we will be held accountable.

Apparently, the "I didn't mean to hurt anyone" defense doesn't hold a lot of weight in God's courtroom.

And this is all assuming, of course, that our words really were reckless, that they really weren't intended to hurt and the harm they caused was truly accidental.

How often is that really the case?

But whether our words are intended to hurt or just happen to, my point is that they can hurt a lot more people than they used to be able to.

---

[3] The NIV has "empty" here which is a literal rendering of the Greek *argos,* but I have changed it to "careless" following the tradition of other translations like the NASB and the ESV. It is clear that Matthew used *argos* here in the sense of "without intentional direction", a concept well-expressed by the English word "careless."

The printing press amplified more voices to a listening world than anyone before Gutenberg could have ever imagined.

The internet and social media apps have now accomplished the same thing for nearly everyone on the planet.

Words have always been powerful, but now everyone's words have legs that carry them out of the home, across the street, and around the world.

There has never been a time that paying careful attention to our words has been more important than it is today.

24

3 - The Most ~~Dangerous~~ Powerful Part of Your Body

I originally intended to call this book *Your Tongue and How To Use It: A User's Guide to the Most Dangerous Part of Your Body*, but some wise friends convinced me that was too provocative a title because it has an inherent sexual overtone to it.

I think they're right and, for the record, I'm glad they spoke up. But at the same time, there's a part of me that feels like my original title wasn't just more engaging, it was more biblical.

The Bad News

The Bible uses some pretty strong words to describe dangerous potential of our tongues:

> **The tongue also is a fire, a world of evil among the parts of the body. It corrupts the whole body, sets the whole course of one's life on fire, and is itself set on fire by hell. All kinds of animals, birds, reptiles and sea creatures are being tamed and have been tamed by mankind, but no human being can tame the tongue. It is a restless evil, full of deadly poison.**
>
> *- James, 3:6-8*

There is no other part of the body the Bible calls attention to with such fiery rhetoric.

I'm not saying there are no other dangerous parts of your body. I'm just saying they all pale in comparison to what the tongue can do.

Nothing else even comes close.

Remember, it was the *words* of Hitler that led to the slaughter of over 6 million Jewish people in WWII, not just because of what he told his generals to do but because of the culture his words created.

It was *words* – in the form of hate speech and propaganda broadcast on the radio – that led to almost a million Tutsis being killed in Rwanda in 1994.

It was mean words on the internet – cyber-bullying we've come to call it - that led Amanda Todd to take her own life in 2012.

The greatest evils visited *upon* the world always begin with words spoken *into* the world.

Which is ironic, if you think about it, because the world that is so negatively impacted by evil's words was also *created* by words.

In the Genesis account of creation, each of God's creative acts was produced by His words. His first creative act was particularly interesting:

> **And God said, "Let there be light," and there was light.**
>
> *- Genesis 1:3*

Notice that it's not "and God said" followed by "and then He made". It's "God said" and "there was." This same pattern recurs throughout the account: "God said" followed by "and it was so."

God's word literally created the world

I don't know if you've ever thought about it, but the Bible says the world that was *created* by words was also *corrupted* by them.

Satan's temptation of Eve in the Garden could have taken many forms. He could have plucked the fruit from the tree and put it in her hands, hoping its texture and aroma would entice her. He could have appeared, not as a snake, but as a good-looking hunk of a man, hoping to seduce her into adultery.

But instead, the world was corrupted by words:

> **He said to the woman, "Did God really say, 'You must not eat from any tree in the garden'?"**

- Genesis 3:1

That isn't what God said, of course. God had given Adam and Eve every tree in the Garden *except* the tree of the knowledge of good and evil. And of course, Satan knew that, but his words were carefully formulated to plant a seed of doubt about God's goodness.

When Eve answered that they could eat fruit from the trees in the Garden, she was ostensibly setting the record straight, but she continued on to say:

> **"but God did say, 'You must not eat fruit from the tree that is in the middle of the garden, and you must not touch it, or you will die.'"**

- Genesis 3:3

I keep coming back to that "but God did say" part. But God *did* say.... Am I reading too much into this to detect a hint of doubt on Eve's part? A little touch of "but now that I think about it, that *does* seem a little odd, doesn't it?"

And with the hook set, Satan proceeded to reel her in:

> **"You will not certainly die," the serpent said to the woman.**
>
> **"For God knows that when you eat from it your eyes will be opened, and you will be like God, knowing good and evil."**
>
> **When the woman saw that the fruit of the tree was good for food and pleasing to the eye, and also desirable for gaining wisdom, she took some and ate it. She also gave some to her husband, who was with her, and he ate it.**
>
> *- Genesis 3:4-6*

Of course it was Adam and Eve's action that produced the evil we're still dealing with today, but let's not miss this important fact: The first evil visited *upon* the world began with words spoken *into* the world.

The Good News

Fortunately, our words do not merely have destructive potential. They're not just dangerous. The Bible also says they have the potential to be profoundly good:

> **Gracious words are a honeycomb, sweet to the soul and healing to the bones.**
>
> *- Proverbs 16:24*

Think of Martin Luther King Jr.'s "I Have a Dream" speech.

Or maybe the Gettysburg Address, delivered by President Abraham Lincoln, about which Senator Charles Sumner said, "The battle itself was less important than the speech."

Or maybe someone – a parent, a teacher, a coach – said something to you once that changed the course of your life?

My dad once said to me that he really believed I could be anything I wanted to be.

He was wrong - I'm not good enough with math to be the theoretical physicist I once dreamed of being and the fact that I was wearing contacts at the time meant I couldn't be the F15 fighter pilot I had hoped to become - but I will never forget those words. My dad believed in me and those words gave me a courage and a confidence I still carry with me to this day.

That's the thing about words: like most powerful things, they can have two very different impacts on the world. The Bible makes this very clear:

> **The tongue has the power of life and death, and those who love it will eat its fruit.**
>
> *- Proverbs 18:21*

Here, not only do we have a description of the power of the tongue, we have a prescription. If we love it, that is to say, if we appreciate its power and appropriate it as God intended, that power will not only bless others but bless us as well.

Yet another proverb says:

> **The soothing tongue is a tree of life, but a perverse tongue crushes the spirit.**
>
> *- Proverbs 15:4*

Again, the same power that makes the tongue so dangerous also makes it, potentially, a source of great good.

Could God not have made the tongue, and the words that we cast into the world with it, less powerful? Incapable of dealing death? I assume so, but bereft of such power, we couldn't use it to bring life.

Yes, words can harm, but they can also heal.

They can destroy the fragile sense of worth in a child, but they can also open up a new world of hopeful possibilities for that same child.

Though I know this runs the risk of being hyperbole, I really don't think it is: *it is not possible to overestimate the power of our words.*

Doesn't that mean we better learn how to use them right?

4 - Primum Non Nocere

Primum non nocere.

This is Latin for, "first, do no harm."

You may recognize this as the foundational tenet of medical ethics, originating in the work of Hippocrates who lived in the 5th-century B.C.

What Hippocrates knew is that the first step in making something better is not making it worse.

That's a really important principle to keep in mind if you want to learn to use your words wisely. Because, let's face it: *Words are really hard to take back.*

Have you ever poured out more shampoo than you meant to?

Ever squeezed out more toothpaste than you wanted?

I do a lot of woodwork with epoxy resin that gets poured into voids or around the edges of projects. I spend a lot of time making sure the mold is completely sealed before I pour the epoxy, but every now and then there's a little gap in the caulk and epoxy starts leaking out. I can't even begin to express the panic that sets in as I try to seal up the leak and scoop the epoxy (which is really expensive) back into the mold. It's a crazy-sticky, goopy mess that has ruined a lot more of my work benches and garage floor than I care to admit. Once epoxy gets out, it's almost impossible to put back in.

But words are way worse.

Once they're pushed out into the world, there's no pulling them back. And unlike shampoo or toothpaste, which can at least be rinsed down the drain, words have this unsettling tendency to stick around and keep doing damage.

Because words can't be withdrawn from the world, we have a whole bunch of ways we try to get people to ignore them when they encounter them:

> **"Forget I said that."**
>
> **"I was just kidding."**
>
> **"I didn't mean it like that."**

"Don't take that the wrong way."

"That sounded better in my head."

"It was just a joke."

"I wasn't serious."

"Don't be so sensitive."

These are all ways we try to deal with the inconvenient persistence of our words.

As with any powerful thing, the first key to using our words in a way that helps more than hurts is to make sure they don't have an impact we didn't intend.

Earlier, we looked at Proverbs 12:18 again, which warns us that reckless words are like a sword. But that isn't the whole proverb. Here is the whole thing:

The words of the reckless pierce like swords, but the tongue of the wise brings healing.

- Proverbs 12:18

In the Bible, the defining characteristic of poetry (as opposed to prose) is *parallelism*. What this means is that ancient Hebrew poetry was built on correspondence between elements in different lines.

For example, in this proverb, "words" in the first line corresponds to "tongue" in the second line, and this is a kind of synonymous parallelism in that words are produced by the tongue. Today we might also add "but the tongue – or the thumbs" or, if you're really old school and still type on a keyboard, "or the fingertips".

Likewise, "pierce like swords" in the first line corresponds to "brings healing" in the second. This is a kind of antithetical parallelism.

But consider this: what does "reckless" correspond to?

The answer is "wise". This is another instance of antithetical parallelism, where the first and second terms are, in some way, essentially opposites of each other.

But pay attention to the implication: if the opposite of "reckless" is "wise", then what does that say about the essence of wisdom, at least when it comes to the way they use words?

It says wise people aren't *reckless*, they are *careful*.

So what's the first step to using our words wisely? Being slow and deliberate about which words we let out into the world.

Simply put, we have to be slower to speak. We have to be slower to push our words out into the world. This isn't about being timid or being afraid to speak unpopular truth. This is about making sure what we say is actually what we mean to say and what we should say.

And that usually takes some time.

I know that better than most people, because I work with words for a living. As a pastor, almost everything I do, from preaching messages on the weekend to leading staff throughout the week, comes down to words. And I think most people will tell you that I'm pretty good at my job, which means that I'm pretty good with words.

Some of my skill with words came naturally and some of it was the result of a lot of hard work. But here's the thing: even though I'm pretty good with words, I have learned that I need to give my words time before I push them out into the world or else what they produce will often be different than what I intended.

I usually start working on our sermon series' a year in advance. Then, I start writing a specific message in a series about 6 weeks out. That rough draft gets edited, reviewed, shared with others, and revised at least 6 times before it's delivered.

When I have a meeting with staff or members of the congregation, I usually pray for the Holy Spirit to give me the right words, to give me his words. And I often write down some key things I feel I'm being led to say before the meeting takes place. And then I edit those things a few times to make sure what I'm going to say is what I'm actually supposed to say.

I do the same thing with important conversations with my wife and my kids. I'm not saying I script out every conversation, but I give a lot of thought to how to say certain things that I want to say, whether that's an encouragement or a concern.

Yes, it's a lot of work.

So why do I do it? Because I've learned that reckless rarely represents.

Yes, I like alliteration.

But what I mean here is that reckless words seldom convey what we wanted to convey. Reckless words hurt feelings we never meant to hurt. They raise issues we didn't mean to raise. They cause conversations to turn into conflicts and they turn conflicts into conflagrations.

Why? Two reasons. First, reckless words communicate what didn't need to be said. Second, reckless words fail to communicate what did need to be said. Because they are often poorly chosen, reckless words end up communicating something other than what we intended.

To be fair, reckless words might represent what we're *feeling* in a given moment. They might accurately represent the anger or pain we're experiencing, but they rarely represent the intentions and desires of our better, more considered, selves.

Ironically, reckless words "wreck more" conversations than any other kind of words.

Which is probably why James said:

My dear brothers and sisters, take note of this: Everyone should be quick to listen, slow to speak and slow to become angry, because human anger does not produce the righteousness that God desires.

- James 1:19-20

And it's not just that human anger – and quick words – don't produce the righteousness *God* desires. They also don't produce the results *we* desire...at least when we've cooled off enough to remember that we desire more than just dealing a little damage.

So how do we make sure that our words aren't reckless? Well, James gives us some pretty clear guidance, doesn't he? Everyone should be *quick to listen* and *slow to speak*.

Quick to listen.

Slow to speak.

That's some pretty good advice right there, isn't it?

How often have you responded to something that it turned out you hadn't really understood?

How often have you said something you later regretted, maybe even the second the words were out of your mouth or you clicked the send button?

By the way, some email clients allow you to unsend a message if you do it fast enough. Gmail's default is 5 seconds, which sure doesn't sound a like a lot, but how much of a game-changer would it be if everything that came out of your mouth could be recalled within 5 seconds?!

If we could actually be quick to listen and slow to speak, we'd all have to deal with a lot less fallout from reckless words.

What's the first step of making things better? Don't make it worse. *Primum non nocere*.

So how do we get better at not making things worse?

Here's a few practical ideas:

1. Practice active listening.

We tend to think about listening as a passive activity, but active listening not only improves our listening ability, it also ratchets down the recklessness of our responses. Active listening basically involves giving your full attention to the act of listening and letting the person you're listening to know that's what you're doing.

Internally, this means giving full attention to the person you're listening to. Instead of using the time between your own speaking opportunities to plan what you're going to say, just... listen. Don't plan what you're going to say until they've finished speaking.

Externally, this means letting the person you're listening to know that you're listening. Instead of looking at your phone or something else in the room, maintain eye contact. Use body language like leaning forward or nodding your head to telegraph your commitment to the conversation. Even an occasional "uh huh" or "hmmm" can go a long way.

2. Reflect before you respond.

When it's time to speak, instead of responding to what's been said (or what you think has been said), start by reflecting your understanding back to the speaker. Say things like "so, what you're saying is..." or "if I'm understanding, you feel that..." to put what the speaker has said into your own words. This can go a long way to making sure that, when you do respond, you're responding to what was actually said rather than to a misunderstanding of it.

Another advantage of reflecting is that it gives the other person a chance to correct not only any misunderstanding on *your* part, but also any miscommunication on *their* part. We don't always know *how* to say exactly what we mean. Sometimes, it's not until we know what someone heard that we see how to say what we're trying to say.

3. Identify your emotions.

When it's your turn to speak, before you open your mouth, ask yourself what you're feeling and why.

Are you angry? Hurt? Frustrated?

Or maybe you're excited or even happy?

It's easy to focus only on negative emotions, but I've found that even positive emotions can derail a conversation, especially if what you're excited about ends up communicating something insulting to the other person.

There's an episode of *The Big Bang Theory* where Amy tells her friends that she's "thinking of making one small change" to her appearance. In rapid fire, Penny and Bernadette take turns guessing what change Amy has in mind: "Your clothes?" "Your glasses?" "Your hair?" "Your shoes?" They're obviously happy about her decision, but their happiness ends up steering the conversation in a direction that's pretty negative.

Or imagine two women talking and one says "Steve proposed last night!" and the other responds with, "Oh, that's so great! You've been dating so long, I was starting to wonder what was keeping him from committing to you!" What was intended to be a positive response will almost certainly lead to a loss of confidence for the newly engaged woman.

In addition to identifying your emotions, it's also helpful to identify the source of them. Is what you're feeling a result of something that's come out of the conversation or something your brought in to the conversation?

Taking a moment to identify your feelings can go a long way towards making sure that your feelings aren't running – and probably *ruining* - the conversation. Emotions are good things and they can absolutely help us communicate effectively, but they can also hijack the conversation if they're allowed to operate without being identified.

A little self-reflection not only avoids that danger, it slows down our response time, giving us a little extra space to make sure our words aren't reckless.

And if you need a little added bonus to get you working on being slower to speak, remember this:

> **Even fools are thought wise if they keep silent, and discerning if they hold their tongues.**
>
> *- Proverbs 17:28*

5 - Is It True?

One of the advantages to being slow to speak is that it gives us time to ask a critical question: is what I'm about to say true?

There is probably no way to overestimate the value the Bible places on telling the truth.

Early in the book of Proverbs, we're told that:

There are six things the LORD hates, seven that are detestable to him: haughty eyes, a lying tongue, hands that shed innocent blood, a heart that devises wicked schemes, feet that are quick to

rush into evil, a false witness who pours out lies and a person who stirs up conflict in the community.

- Proverbs 6:16-19

It's interesting to note that, of the seven things God hates, two of them are about lying. And actually, since many scholars think the seventh thing, a person who stirs up conflict in the community, is actually an extension of the false witness, it might be that three of the seven things God hates are related to lying.

Jesus, the Son of God, maintained his Father's intense feelings about lies. In perhaps his harshest criticism of some of the religious leaders of first century Israel, Jesus said:

You belong to your father, the devil, and you want to carry out your father's desires. He was a murderer from the beginning, not holding to the truth, for there is no truth in him. When he lies, he speaks his native language, for he is a liar and the father of lies.

- John 8:44

What Jesus says here is interesting for several reasons. First, he closely associates "not holding to the truth" with being a "murderer". Second, the phrase "from the beginning" is likely a reference to Genesis (the first words of which are "in the beginning"), indicating that the murder Jesus was thinking of took place in the Garden when the devil deceived Adam and Eve. Third, Jesus uses an unusual term for murderer here[4], indicating that he is thinking not of physical murder but of something even worse, the destruction of humanity at a profound and fundamental level which goes beyond the destruction of the body.

If the destruction of humanity in the Garden was accomplished with a lie, it should come as no surprise that its redemption would be accomplished by the truth. And so Jesus said:

> **I am the way and the truth and the life. No one comes to the Father except through me.**
>
> *- John 14:6*

And then, just a few breaths later, Jesus made this promise to his followers:

> **And I will ask the Father, and he will give you another advocate to help you and be with you forever-- the <u>Spirit of truth</u>. The world cannot accept him, because it**

---

[4] The normal Greek term for murderer is *phoneus*, but here, Jesus uses *anthropoktonos* (lit: man-slayer) which occurs only twice in the Bible, here and in 1 John 3:15 where it is said that anyone who "hates a brother or sister is a murderer."

neither sees him nor knows him. But you know him, for he lives with you and will be in you.

- John 14:16-17

If the truth is so central to the story of humanity's destruction and salvation, then clearly, no one who follows Jesus – who is *the* Truth - and who is indwelt by the Spirit *of* truth, has the option of playing fast and loose with truth.

Therefore, before we speak, we must always ask: is this true?

What is truth?

That we must speak truth is non-negotiable. However, before we can ask if a particular thing we're thinking about saying is true, we must first deal with an age-old philosophical debate: *what is truth?*
Let me cut right to the chase. Contrary to what a lot of people seem to think today, we don't get to decide what's true.

Truth is not up to us. There's no "my truth" or "your truth". There's just truth. There's just what is or isn't true.

What is *truth*? What does it mean for something to be true or, for that matter, false?

I realize this is a long-standing philosophical debate. Almost 2,000 years ago, the Roman governor Pontius Pilate, responding to Jesus's claim that "everyone on the side of truth listens to me" (John 18:37), replied with a question philosophers are still asking today: "What is truth?" (John 18:38).

Look, I like philosophy as much as the next person. Actually, I probably like it more. I enjoy talking about things like whether or not a tree that falls in a forest when there's no one around to hear it actually makes a sound.

But, in my opinion, the question of what makes something true just isn't that complex: *Something is true if it corresponds with reality. Something is false if it doesn't correspond with reality.*

Technically speaking, this is what's known as the *Correspondence Theory* of truth. It depends on three assumptions:

1. **There is an objective reality that exists independent of human thoughts, beliefs, or perceptions.** In other words, we don't create the world we live in by what we think, believe or perceive. If Bigfoot exists, it exists even if no one believes it does, and if it does not exist, it does not matter how many people believe it exists. Their belief will not bring Bigfoot into existence.

2. **Our words can accurately represent or describe this objective reality.** This does not necessarily mean that our words are entirely adequate to completely

represent reality. For instance, no matter how exhaustively we attempt to describe what it is like to jump into a cold lake on a hot day, our words will never be able to completely capture such an experience. But, just because we cannot describe something fully does not mean that we cannot accurately describe something in part.

3. **The truth value of our words is determined by correspondence or alignment between reality and the words which claim to represent that reality.** Technically speaking, statements like "the water is cold", "I did not commit that crime," or "God exists" are *truth claims*. They are statements which claim to accurately describe reality, and their truth value (i.e. whether they are true or false) is determined by whether or not they do, in fact, accurately describe reality in the way they claim to.

Think about it like this: As I am writing these words, the world is processing something shocking that happened at a political rally in Pennsylvania.

To keep it simple, let's reduce what people are claiming about what happened to two primary options:

- Some people are claiming Former President Trump survived an attempted assassination attempt.
- Some people are claiming the whole thing was staged to make Former President Trump look like a hero.

Which claim is true?

The answer is: whichever claim corresponds/aligns with what actually took place. Either there was a legitimate attempt to kill former President Trump or there was not.

Truth is all about alignment with reality.

Can we know truth?

Now here's where things get complicated.

It might not be hard to get most people to agree that a claim is true *if* it aligns with reality, but getting everyone to agree *that* a claim aligns with reality is a lot harder.

In other words, what's complicated about truth isn't *defining* it, but *discerning* it. Just because we know *what truth is*, generally, doesn't mean we know *what is true*, specifically.

Take the case of what happened at the rally in Pennsylvania.

Personally, I do believe someone attempted to assassinate former President Trump. I think the "evidence" strongly supports that claim. But those who claim it was staged have "evidence" they're pointing to as well.

And here's where things get complicated, because how we know what is true is a much more complex question than how we know what truth is.

Here's an interesting exercise:

> 1. Grab a piece of paper and write down ten things you believe to be true. Make them from a variety of areas in your life: your faith, your relationships, politics, etc.
>
> 2. Now, next to each belief, on a scale from 1 to 10, rate your confidence level that each belief is true, that it aligns with reality.
>
> 3. Finally, next to each belief, write down how you came to that belief.

When I do this exercise with people, a lot of them are surprised to find that some of the beliefs they are most confident about are also the ones they have the hardest time explaining the origins of.

But this isn't all that surprising, if you think about it.

We like to believe that we're rational creatures, but the truth is, a lot of our beliefs aren't rooted in rational consideration of evidence. Some of our beliefs are based on the beliefs of those we grew up with or are surrounded by. Others are based on something we heard that just jived with our experience, our self-perception, or with other beliefs. And yes, some of them are based on rational consideration of evidence.

In the same way that truth doesn't depend on what you believe or how much you believe it, truth also doesn't depend on how you *came* to believe it.

If you believe something because your parents believed it and that belief lines up with reality, your belief is true. If you believe it because your parents believed it, but that belief doesn't line up with reality, your belief is false.

If you believe something because you rationally considered a lot of evidence, and that belief lines up with reality, your belief is true. But if it turns out there was a lot of evidence you hadn't considered which shows your belief doesn't line up with reality, guess what? Your belief is false.

How we come to believe what we believe is a complicated subject that we don't have the time to get into here. So why am I bringing it up at all?

Because I think it's important to admit that some of what we believe might be wrong.

Have you ever been wrong?

I have, more times than I like to admit, but I have to admit it because this admission sets the stage for an important principle about speaking wisely: *to speak wisely, we must maintain a certain amount of open-mindedness.*

By the way, what I'm calling open-mindedness is often called *humility*, but I prefer not to use that term. Humility is a relational characteristic related to the willingness to put others before yourself. It doesn't necessarily have anything to do with truth or with the level of certainty we have that our beliefs are true.

Think about Jesus:

> **Do nothing out of selfish ambition or vain conceit. Rather, in humility value others above yourselves, not looking to your own interests but each of you to the interests of the others. In your relationships with one another, have the same mindset as Christ Jesus: Who, being in very nature God, did not consider equality with God something to be used to his own advantage; rather, he made himself nothing by taking the very nature of a servant, being made in human likeness. And being found in appearance as a man, he humbled himself by becoming obedient to death-- even death on a cross!**
>
> *- Philippians 2:3-8*

Clearly, Jesus was humble, having been willing to sacrifice himself to save us. But none of his teaching started with, "Ok, now I'm not really sure if this is true or not, but here's something that might – or maybe might not – be useful to think about."

Jesus was 100% humble and 100% certain.

Likewise, we can be humble and certain or self-centered and uncertain.

What this means is that humility and certainty/confidence are actually unrelated concepts.

What we often call *humility* - meaning that a person is willing to acknowledge that their beliefs, however strongly held at the moment, may not prove to be true in the end – is, I think, simply *wisdom*. It really has nothing to do with being other-centered which is the true meaning of humility.

A wise person forms their beliefs carefully. A wise person gathers evidence and truly considers various ways that evidence can be accounted for. A wise person talks with others – and especially others who hold alternate views – before deciding what he or she thinks about a subject.

This is why the Bible constantly describes the wise as listeners:

> **let the wise listen and add to their learning, and let the discerning get guidance—**
>
> *- Proverbs 1:5*
>
> **Listen to my instruction and be wise; do not disregard it. Blessed are those who listen to me, watching daily at my doors, waiting at my doorway.**
>
> *- Proverbs 8:33-34*

The wise store up knowledge, but the mouth of a fool invites ruin.

- Proverbs 10:14

By virtue of the very process by which a truly wise person forms their beliefs, a wise person also holds those beliefs, once formed, with a certain amount of open-mindedness. A wise person knows that it is always possible that they have not yet considered all of the relevant evidence in forming their beliefs. A wise person knows that they may encounter additional evidence in the future which will require a re-evaluation of those beliefs.

A lot of people used to be quite confident the world was flat.

The world's best scientists were once certain that living organisms could spontaneously arise from non-living matter.

Doctors once believed that disease was caused by "bad air" and even washing your hands before performing surgery was a complete waste of time.

We've been wrong a lot and wise people keep this in mind as they are both forming their beliefs and speaking to others about them.

Does this mean that being wise means never being confident about our beliefs? Not at all. To be wise isn't to be wishy-washy, it's to be unwavering in our commitment to truth but also to recognize that our perception of the truth may still be in process.

Does this mean that being wise means we should just assume what we believe is wrong?

Not at all.

It just means that we speak to – and listen to – those who think we're wrong very differently.

The Bible says that one characteristic of fools is that they are so confident in their beliefs that they feel no need to listen to anyone else:

> **The way of fools seems right to them, but the wise listen to advice.**
>
> *- Proverbs 12:15*

Notice that it doesn't say that the wise necessarily *take* the advice they're given, but they listen to it. Why? Because the wise know that there's always a chance that they still have something to learn.

Fools, on the other hand, have no interest in the possibility of learning. Rather, the Bible says:

> **Fools find no pleasure in understanding but delight in airing their own opinions.**
>
> *- Proverbs 18:2*

Being wise means we really listen to those who believe differently than we do. And when I say *listen*, I'm not talking about listening in order to prepare our rebuttal. Rather, I mean listening with genuine curiosity and openness to the possibility that we will learn something.

Being open-minded also means that we should avoid speaking with hubris (a great and much under-used term from the ancient Greeks which means excessive self-confidence).

As confident as you might be, sometimes you're going to be very confident and wrong.

And that's ok. You don't have to apologize for being wrong, just make sure you don't have to apologize for the way you acted when you thought you were right.

Echo Chambers

If you don't know what an echo chamber is, the term was first coined by Cass Sunstein, a law professor at Harvard Law School, to describe a situation where people are exposed only to information and opinions that reinforce their own views.

The idea is that people who only watch CNN because they tend to agree with the editorial slant of the organization, only hear that particular editorial slant. Likewise, people who only listen to Fox News because of its editorial slant only hear that particular editorial slant. They are, in essence, putting themselves in a chamber where they only hear echoes of their own opinions.

Over time, echo chambers increase our confidence in our beliefs, but they do so, in part, by limiting our exposure to alternative perspectives and the evidential basis for those perspectives.

Think about it: how often do you think gun-control advocates are actually reading and considering arguments from thoughtful gun-rights advocates? How often do Republicans read or listen to left-leaning political outlets? How often to Democrats listen to right-leaning political outlets?

The truth is, most of us only know what "the other side" says because of sound-bites we pick up while listening to sources that are on "our side."

Now, echo chambers are nothing new. They have always existed.

I doubt very much that the Spartans were going into the agora in Athens on a regular basis to understand the nuances of Athenian perspective. No, Spartans listened to Spartans and Athenians listened to Athenians. That's an echo chamber.

Echo chambers have been around for a long time.

What has changed more recently is the fact that many of our echo chambers are now invisible. What I mean is, we are trapped in them simply because we don't even know that we're in them. Consequently, we believe the messages we hear in them are evidence rather than echoes.

On some level, if you only watch Fox News or CNN, you know you're in an echo chamber. You know there are major news outlets coming from a completely different perspective. You may choose not to engage with those outlets, but at least you know you're choosing not to engage.

You used to know you were in an echo chamber.

But social media has created echo chambers we have no idea we're trapped in.

On the surface, social media platforms like Facebook or TikTok seem like the opposite of echo chambers. After all, they're not curated by an editorial staff. Anyone can post anything, so we aren't only seeing posts from a particular perspective.

We're getting unrestricted access to every perspective, right?

Wrong.

A few months ago, I ran across a video on TikTok made by someone who believes the earth is flat. And I watched it several times, not because I found it persuasive, but because I was just so fascinated by the existence of this belief in an era where we have thousands of actual images of the round ball we live on.

Over the next few days, more and more flat earth videos came across my feed. And I watched them, because I was fascinated that they existed!

But the more I watched them, the more of them the TikTok algorithm fed me.

Pretty soon, flat earth videos were most of what TikTok was sending me.

What was the impact of that on me?

Well, I'm now convinced that the world is a flat disc.

Just kidding! No, that didn't happen. But what did happen was I started to believe there were a LOT more people who believed in a flat earth than I would have ever thought possible. How else could I explain the massive number of videos I kept running across?

The flat earth community has to be huge, right?

Wrong.

Because I had watched these videos for longer than other videos, the TikTok algorithm, which is designed to keep you on the platform as long as possible, started sending me more and more of the videos it knew I was willing to watch.

This left me with the impression that Tiktok, and by extension, the world, was *filled* with people who believe in a flat earth.

In essence, the TikTok algorithm had created an echo chamber which was distorting my view of reality by curating what videos I saw and what videos I didn't.

This happens all the time without people being aware of it. If you click on that highly conservative political post on Facebook, the Meta algorithm says, "Ok, she likes posts that contain these key words. Here's a bunch more of them!"

The impression this gives is that nearly everyone thinks this way and therefore, those who don't are a relatively small minority trying to seize disproportionate influence in our society.

One of the most interesting — and alarming — findings of the study that was presented in the documentary *The Social Dilemma* is that the echo chambers created by social media are substantially altering our ability to have productive civil discourse.

Then there's the *illusory truth effect*, which causes people to believe information is true simply because of repeated exposures to it. The fact that the algorithms are showing us certain stories or claims over and over again predisposes us to believe those stories or claims even when, in fact, they have no basis in reality.

And let's be clear: it's not just social media platforms.

I use Google News as well as Microsoft's Bing to stay up to date on current events, but the kinds of articles I click on (and the searches I make in their respective search engines) have an obvious impact on the kinds of news stories it suggests I read.

And don't even get me started on the interrelationship between various tech platforms. Recently I used Google on my phone to search for something specific about a laser engraver and the next time I pulled up YouTube on my Apple TV, guess what kinds of videos my recommendation feed was filled with? You guessed it: laser engravers.

So does this means we can't believe *anything* we see? No, it just means we need to be careful about believing *everything* we see.

More and more, what we see is being curated by algorithms that are designed to show us only what we *want* to see.

To be clear, this isn't nefarious. It's just commercial. Those algorithms are designed to keep you on the platforms for as long as possible because that's how those platforms make their money. TikTok wasn't trying to convince me the world is flat...it just wanted me to stay on as long as it could keep me.

And if we're going to be cautious about what we see, we also need to be cautious about what we say based on what we've seen. There's a pretty good chance that what we've been allowed to see in our echo chambers isn't all there is to see in the wider world.

Breaking Out of Our Echo Chambers

While modern technology creates echo chambers, it also gives us the tools to break out of them. We just have to be intentional about it.
I have found it very helpful to ask the question "is this true?" of nearly every claim I encounter. The moment I read or hear something that elicits a reaction in me, either positive or negative, I commit to doing at least a little research to find out of it's true before I share it with anyone.

This might sound daunting, but we live in a golden age of research. The amount of information available to us online is staggering, and our ability to access it anywhere, anytime would be almost impossible to describe to previous generations.

To be fair, the shear amount of information can be overwhelming, and the presence of conflicting sources can make us skeptical about discerning the truth. However recent advances in AI technology have made it much easier to sort through all the data and get relatively reliable information in a short amount of time.

Still, it will sometimes be the case that, when you research something you've heard, you will not be able to conclusively answer the question, "is this true?" Some issues are so complex or the evidence so contradictory, that you simply won't be able to come to a confident conclusion.

So what do you do when you can't be confident something is true? You have two options: don't say it or, at least, acknowledge your uncertainty.

If you aren't very confident it's true, you should be very cautious about sharing it.

6 - Tasty Truth

To speak in a way that builds up rather than tears down is to speak in a way that honors God and respects the inherent value of human beings.

Most Christians reading this book will probably agree that honoring God is a non-negotiable. As followers of Jesus, we absolutely have to check that box when we speak. But I think what we can forget is that it's our ability to check the second box – respecting the inherent value of human beings – that often determines whether or not we're actually honoring God.

One of the most inconvenient things Jesus ever said was this:

By this everyone will know that you are my disciples, if you love one another.

- John 13:35

I think a lot of Christians wish he had said everyone would know we are his disciples by our understanding of doctrine. Or by the political party we belong to. Or even just the sins we avoid.

Unfortunately, Jesus made it all about how we treat one another.

Of course, that doesn't mean that doctrine doesn't matter, that politics are meaningless, or that sin is insignificant. But it does mean that honoring God isn't just about what we say to or about God. It's also about what we say to and about those made in His image.

Here's how the Bible puts it:

With the tongue we praise our Lord and Father, and with it we curse human beings, who have been made in God's likeness. Out of the same mouth come praise and cursing. My brothers and sisters, this should not be.

- James 3:9-10

Simply put, we cannot honor God and dishonor those He created. The two activities are fundamentally incompatible.

Think about it like this: if someone said to you, "I love you, but I hate your daughter," would you feel loved? Probably not. To love someone is also to love those they love. As angy

This is why Jesus said:

> **"You have heard that it was said to the people long ago, 'You shall not murder, and anyone who murders will be subject to judgment.' But I tell you that anyone who is angry with a brother or sister will be subject to judgment. Again, anyone who says to a brother or sister, 'Raca,' is answerable to the court. And anyone who says, 'You fool!' will be in danger of the fire of hell.**
>
> **Therefore, if you are offering your gift at the altar and there remember that your brother or sister has something against you, leave your gift there in front of the altar. First go and be reconciled to them; then come and offer your gift."**
>
> *- Matthew 5:21-24*

Why is cursing someone – or calling them a fool – such a big deal to God?

It's because, as James says, human beings were created "in God's likeness."

It's easy to misunderstand what this means and, therefore, to fail to understand why James brings it up in the context of how we speak to and about other human beings.

In English, the word "likeness" conveys to us a sense of similarity, so we naturally assume what James is saying is that human beings resemble God. But that's actually not what he's saying at all.

What James says here is actually a call for his audience to remember the creation account of Genesis 1 and what God said about human beings there:

> **Then God said, "Let us make mankind in our image, in our likeness, so that they may rule over the fish in the sea and the birds in the sky, over the livestock and all the wild animals, and over all the creatures that move along the ground."**
>
> **So God created mankind in his own image, in the image of God he created them; male and female he created them. God blessed them and said to them, "Be fruitful and increase in number; fill the earth and subdue it. Rule over the fish in the sea and**

the birds in the sky and over every living creature that moves on the ground."

- Genesis 1:26-28

Notice there are two terms God uses here related to the purpose of the human beings He was creating: image and likeness.

In English, both of those terms convey a sense of similarity or resemblance, but in the original Hebrew, this sense is much less evident. In Hebrew, both of these terms are more about *representation* than *resemblance*. In other words, both of these terms were used to denote physical objects that represented – or served as a kind of stand-in – for someone or something that wasn't physically present.

You might be surprised to learn that the Hebrew term (*ts'lem*) translated here as "image" was used at times in the Bible to speak of "idols." Does that mean God made human beings as his *idols*?

Well, sort of.

You see, in the ancient world, an idol was a physical object that *represented* a spirit. Ancient people didn't think the objects – statues or whatnot – actually were the gods or goddesses they worshipped. What they believed was these idols, these "images," *represented* those spirits in the physical world we inhabit. They also believed those spirits manifested their presence in the world through those physical objects that represented them.

When we understand this, what God says about human beings in Genesis 1 becomes far clearer and far more significant.

Having created a physical world, God created a physical being to represent Him and to manifest His presence in the physical world: human beings.

This is some fairly deep theology and I've written about it in far more depth in an earlier book,[5] but for now, all we need to understand is this: to be made in the image or likeness of God is to be made with the profound purpose of representing God Himself in His creation.

Now, of course, because of sin we don't do that well...or even understand that we were made for this profound purpose. But neither our lack of awareness of our purpose nor the poor job we often do in fulfilling our purpose, changes the existence of that purpose or the value of human beings because of that purpose.

Think about it like this: imagine the government of another country mistreated an American tourist. That would be a big deal, obviously, but what if that government did the same thing to the American ambassador to that country? Much bigger deal, right? But why? Because the attack on the U.S. ambassador, who represents the U.S. nation, essentially constitutes an attack on the U.S. itself.

---

[5] The book is called *The Kingdom For the Kingless: Learning to Live as Ambassadors of the Now-and-Coming King*.

This is why we cannot honor God and dishonor human beings. This is why the two things are inextricably linked. This is why James says we cannot praise our Father and curse human beings. This is why Jesus says anyone who says "you fool" will be "in danger of hell." We are not just mistreating citizens, we are mistreating ambassadors. Our affront is not simply to those we speak against but to the God who created them to represent Him and manifest His presence in creation.

It might also be useful to think about how we treat the American flag. There are strict rules about how the flag is to be treated. Why is that? Because the fabric and the dye are so valuable? No, because of what the fabric and dye *represent*.

It's ironic that some of the people who are most enraged by mistreatment of the U.S. flag are the least bothered by cursing, insulting and otherwise maligning human beings who represent something much more sacred than a nation.

Truth and Kindness

So what does it take to honor God and those made in His image?

In the interest of keeping it simple, let's just start here: *To honor God and others, everything we say has to be both true and kind.*

Not either true OR kind, both true AND kind.

If anything that comes out of our mouth is one but not the other, what's coming out of our mouth isn't going to honor God and those made in His image.

The Bible makes an interesting statement about conversation:

> **Let your conversation be always full of grace, seasoned with salt, so that you may know how to answer everyone.**

- Colossians 4:6

That's a slightly odd metaphor, isn't it? Since when do we salt our conversations? But it's a powerful metaphor, isn't it? Because we all know what salt does, don't we?

Salt makes things taste better.

Have you ever had French fries without salt? They're terrible.

Do you know why so much restaurant food tastes better than what we make at home? Restaurants use a LOT more salt than we usually do at home.

Putting aside any consideration of how much salt is too much salt and any concerns about how salt can raise your blood pressure, the bottom line is that salt makes things taste better! It's undeniable.

And they knew it all the way back in the first century.

So what the Bible is saying is that grace makes our words tastier.

But it's not just our words it makes tastier. As we'll see below, there is no grace without truth, so grace makes the truth tasty.

Grace is what makes the truth palatable enough to be considered, to be heard, to be understood, to be acknowledged, to be dealt with. That's what the Bible means when it says we're supposed to let our conversations be always full of grace, *seasoned with salt*.

By the way, if you don't know what grace is, let me define it for you: *grace is undeserved kindness*. It's the willingness to be kind to someone even when, at least by the world's standards, what they've done justifies retribution or revenge.

In my mind, *grace* is different than *mercy*, though the two terms are often used interchangeably. The way I see it, *mercy* is withholding the negative consequences someone deserves, but *grace* goes above and beyond, giving something good to someone who doesn't deserve it.

Jesus was describing grace when he said:

> **"But to you who are listening I say: Love your enemies, do good to those who hate you, bless those who curse you, pray for those who mistreat you."**
>
> *- Luke 6:27-28*

I find it fascinating that Jesus starts off with "but to you who are listening." Isn't he speaking to people who were already listening? It's almost as if he's saying, "Ok, look, I know you're going to want to tune me out when I say this, but don't do it!"

Of course, the reason we're so tempted to tune him out here is that what he says is so counter-cultural.

Actually, it's not just counter-*cultural*, it's counter-*sensical*. It's so contrary to how the world teaches us to act that it feels like it makes no sense at all. And even Christians who most of us would call committed followers of Jesus sometimes look at that and think, "that almost sounds like a dangerous mistake, Jesus!"

I know that happens because I've had people come up to me after messages on that passage and say "I feel like you're taking that too literally" or "sure...but don't we have to be careful about taking that too far?"

Do we?

Did Jesus leave us with that option?

If he did, I have yet to find it.

Of course, the reason we all struggle with what Jesus said here is just that there's something in us that balks at the idea of being kind to those who don't deserve it.

But that's what grace is: undeserved kindness.

What's interesting to me about grace is that it cannot exist without truth.

Why do I say that? Because giving good to those who don't deserve it starts with recognizing that they don't deserve it. It starts with acknowledging *why* they don't deserve it.

Grace requires an honest, objective realization that what they've done was wrong, that what they've done was hurtful, that what they've done was cruel....and then choosing to respond with kindness in spite of that objective evaluation.

That's why there is no grace without truth.

The Bible says:

> **But God demonstrates his own love for us in this: While we were still sinners, Christ died for us.**
>
> *- Romans 5:8*

Notice it's not *while we were still ignorant*. It's not *while we were still making mistakes, but we really didn't know any better*. No, it's while we were still *sinners*. While we were still deliberately crossing the line and missing the mark.

That's a pretty blunt evaluation of who we were, but it's true.

And that's what makes what God did *grace*.

There is no grace without truth. But...grace is what makes that truth tasty.

7 - Is It Kind?

If the God who saved us because of his grace insists that we treat others with grace, and if grace is undeserved kindness, then what we say has to be both *true*, and *kind*.

We've talked about what truth is. Now let's talk about kindness. What does it mean to be kind?

Well, first, let's get a common, but mistaken idea out of the way: being kind isn't the same thing as being nice.

We often use the two words synonymously, but I think they're very different and it's important to understand the difference.

As I'm using the term, *nice* is about maintaining harmony and avoiding conflict at the expense of truth.

There's nothing inherently wrong with keeping the peace. The Bible actually says that pursing harmony and avoiding unnecessary conflict is a good thing:

> **It is to one's honor to avoid strife, but every fool is quick to quarrel.**
>
> - Proverbs 20:3

> **As charcoal to embers and as wood to fire, so is a quarrelsome person for kindling strife.**
>
> - Proverbs 26:21

The problem is when avoiding conflict comes at the expense of truth, and especially when we avoid speaking the truth because a lie is easier on us.

The Bible has another interesting proverb that addresses this:

> **Have I not written thirty sayings for you, sayings of counsel and knowledge, teaching you to be honest and to speak the truth, so that you bring back truthful reports to those you serve?**
>
> - Proverbs 22:20-21

Why would anyone not bring back truth to "those you serve?" If you're serving someone by reporting back to them, why would you even be tempted not to tell them the truth?

Have you ever heard the phrase "don't shoot the messenger?"

Do you know what that's saying?

Because people tend to get mad at the messenger.

In other words, people tend to have a hard time separating the message from the messenger who brings it. And when the message isn't to their liking, they tend to take it out on the person who brought it.

Which creates a pretty strong motive for not speaking the truth if you think the truth isn't going to be well-received. So instead of speaking the truth, you lie.

But why?

Because it's best for the person you serve? No, because it's easier for *you*.

If you told them the truth, they might get mad at you, but if you fudged the truth a little, if you withheld the truth a bit…if you lied, well, that would make things a lot easier on you, wouldn't it?

So instead of telling the truth, you tell them what they want to hear…or at least don't tell them what you know they don't want to hear.

That's nice. You only tell people what they want to hear.

Unfortunately, nice is ultimately self-serving, and it comes at a cost to the person we're being nice to.

You cannot really serve people by being nice.

Nice says to the toddler who wants dino-nuggets instead of a well-balanced meal, "fine, I'll put some in the microwave." That's not what's best for the toddler, but it's what's easiest for the parent.

Nice says to your coworker, who wanted you to proofread his report before giving it to your boss, "Looks good!" even though you know it doesn't address what your boss was asking for.

Nice tolerates the drunk man at a party and smiles at his sexist jokes. Extremely nice people don't even roll their eyes or gossip to their friends about the guy after he's passed out on the couch. Because they're so *nice*.

Kind, on the other hand, is about showing genuine care for someone, even if it comes at the cost of the one showing kindness.

Kind says to the toddler, "This is what I fixed for you because it's better for you," even though you know there's going to be a tantrum and a battle of wills.

Kind says to your coworker, "I know you put a lot of time into this, but I'm afraid it's missing a couple of things I know the boss was looking for" even though you know you're going to have to stay late to help him get it ready for submission.

Kind takes the drunk man aside and says "If you keep this up, you're going to embarrass your friends and hate yourself tomorrow. I don't want to see that happen. Let me take you to get a cup of coffee and get you home to sleep it off."

Nice is superficial and self-serving. *Kind* is deep and self-sacrificing. *Nice* does what's easiest for me, *kind* does what's best for you.

Nice is cheap. Kind is costly.

Interestingly, the word *nice* derives from the Latin *nescius* which originally meant "ignorant." Over time, it evolved into the Old French *nice*, which meant "timid".

It doesn't take any courage to be nice.

Kind, on the other hand, derives from the Old English and proto-Germanic *cynn* or *kin* which means "family."

Nice is timid, refusing to speak the truth because it might create an uncomfortable situation, but in so doing nice treats other people without respect.

Kind is courageous, treating others like family, even when doing so is inconvenient and requires personal sacrifice.

The 4 C's of Kindness

Before we speak, we have to ask: is it true?

But we also have to ask: is it kind?

How do we know if something is truly kind?

First, kindness requires *compassion*, which is basically looking at another human being and seeing them as a fellow human being. Kindness knows that we've been hurt by other people's words and wants to avoid doing the same thing to others as much as possible.

But kindness also seeks the best for others and knows that sometimes we have to say things that are *for* their good but don't *feel* good.

Therefore, second, kindness is also *careful*. Kindness is careful how it says things because it knows that what we say will cause others to feel something. Kindness works to cause as little hurt, pain, disappointment or frustration as possible in the pursuit of the other person's good.

Third, kindness is *clear*. Kindness knows that ambiguity is often more painful than specificity. We sometimes default to vagueness because it feels less personal, but it usually leaves the other person with nothing definite to address. Kindness gives specifics so that the person can actually do something with what you've said to them.

Finally, kindness is *costly*. Kindness rarely stops with a critique, but often offers a commitment on the part of the speaker. It doesn't simply say "do better", it says "I'm here to help."

8 – The Four Worlds

If words create worlds, then the kinds of worlds we create depend on the kinds of words we speak.

The Bible describes several different kinds of words and, by extension, several different kinds of worlds they create, but they can all be classified on the basis of the two questions we've already considered.

Is it true?

Is it kind?

IS IT TRUE?

	NO	YES
IS IT KIND? YES	FLATTERY	GRACE
IS IT KIND? NO	SLANDER	GOSSIP

Flattery

Flattery is untrue, but it is kind...at least on the surface. The better word is actually "nice". We talked about the difference between nice and kind in the last chapter.

Flattery is saying something that isn't true, but it's ostensibly intended to make the other person feel good.

And the Bible isn't...well, very *flattering* about this kind of speech, in part because it ultimately hurts those it is at least pretending to be kind to:

A lying tongue hates those it hurts, and a flattering mouth works ruin.

- Proverbs 26:28

When Coletta and I were first married, I was working hard at getting her parents to like me and, as a result, I was often nice rather than kind. One Christmas they brought me a brick of cheese from an Amish farm near where they live. Now, when I say "brick", I mean that quite literally. It was enormous!

Now, I liked it. I like most cheese and this was good cheese. So of course, I thanked them for it. Actually, because I wanted them to like me, I went a little overboard in thanking them and telling them how much I loved the cheese. In my attempt to get them to like me, I went past the truth into something less than the truth.

That's flattery.

So guess what they brought me the next time they came for a visit? And guess what I did? I went overboard again about how much I loved the cheese...and as soon as they were gone, I put the second brick in the freezer next to the first brick which I had only eaten maybe a quarter of by that point.

Why didn't I tell them I hadn't finished the first brick? Because I was being nice...which was easier on me. I would have been embarrassed because I had told them how much I LOVED the cheese but hadn't actually eaten very much of it. It was easier on me to just keep up the act and put the cheese in the freezer.

Guess what they brought the next time they came to visit? And the next time? And the next time? Eventually, I had enough bricks of cheese in my freezer to start a construction project!

My flattery wasn't good for anyone. My in-laws spent money that was ultimately wasted and my freezer was filled with a guilt-inducing amount of cheese that kept me anxious every time my in-laws were in town.

The Bible also says that flattery, while it's intended to garner favor, actually works against that end:

> **Whoever rebukes a person will in the end gain favor rather than one who has a flattering tongue.**
>
> *- Proverbs 28:23*

The simple fact is that untruth, regardless of motive, does not provide a suitable relational foundation to build upon.

Gossip

Gossip is true, but it's unkind.

We often think about gossip as being untrue. There's an episode of The Office where Michael spreads several lies in the hopes that people will not believe the one true thing he accidentally made public. At one point in the episode, Jim says "It's just gossip" meaning it's untrue.

But he's wrong. The biblical word for something that's untrue and unkind is slander. We'll get to that in a bit.

But for now, it's important to understand that gossip is actually true, it just shouldn't have been shared:

A gossip betrays a confidence, but a trustworthy person keeps a secret.

- Proverbs 11:13

A gossip betrays a confidence; so avoid anyone who talks too much.

- Proverbs 20:19

Notice that in both of these very similar proverbs, a gossip betrays a *confidence*. What is a confidence? It's a mutual trust created by someone sharing something vulnerable with another person or persons in the expectation that they will keep that information confined to that circle of trust.

No one takes another into their confidence by sharing a lie. A confidence is created when something true and vulnerable is shared. But a gossip breaks that confidence by sharing that truth with others.

Essentially, gossip is making public what should have been kept private.

The Bible actually uses three different words for gossips. In English, I think of them as:

The Informer Gossip (Hebrew: *rakil*)

These are the people who just love having information not everyone else has…and letting everyone know that they're in the know by sharing this information.

The Informer Gossip isn't necessarily out to hurt someone, they're just out to get people to pay attention to them. But in this self-centered pursuit, they aren't being kind.

The harm they do may be accidental, but that doesn't make it and less hurtful. In the end, the Informer tears down trust and builds a wall out of the rubble, ruining the relationship.

The Backroom Whisperer Gossip (Hebrew: *ragan*)

These are people who have information about someone else, usually damaging, that they share with others for the purpose of tearing that person down.

Sometimes we do this because we're jealous. I've been guilty of that. I found out once that a certain pastor of a very large church built a multi-million dollar home and I told a few people what I found out. It was entirely true, but if I'm brutally honest with myself, it was because I was jealous of the other pastor and it made me feel better to make other people think worse of that pastor. That was gossip. That was the Backroom Whisperer in me coming out.

We might also become a Backroom Whisperer kind of gossip because we're in competition with someone and a little damaging information leaked to the right person will keep them from getting something we want for ourselves.

The Blabber Mouth Gossip (Hebrew: *pathah*)

The Hebrew *pathah* literally means "wide open" and is used to describe a person who isn't careful with what comes out of their mouths.

It's not necessarily that they're trying to cause harm to someone else or even trying to make themselves look better...they're just not careful about what they say.

What makes gossip so attractive, and therefore so dangerous, is just that it's so delectable.

Imagine being in a meeting at work and the sales manager says, "All right team, earnings for the third quarter are down about 2% and we have the departmental reviews coming up so we need to double down this week and, oh, by the way, Ted's wife left him last weekend, so let's all try to cut him as much slack as we can, ok?" Forget about percentages and sales quotas and upcoming reviews... what fact are you going to be focused on?

That's why the Bible says:

> **The words of a gossip are like choice morsels; they go down to the inmost parts.**
>
> *- Proverbs 18:8*

The problem is that what's going down isn't actually a choice morsel, it's poison. The Bible actually calls it evil and puts it in the same company with some pretty terrible stuff:

> **They have become filled with every kind of wickedness, evil, greed and depravity. They are full of envy, murder, strife, deceit and malice. They are gossips, slanderers, God-haters, insolent, arrogant and boastful; they invent ways of doing evil; they disobey their parents; they have no understanding, no fidelity, no love, no mercy. Although they know God's righteous decree that those who do such things deserve death, they not only continue to do these very things but also approve of those who practice them.**

- Romans 1:29-32

Yikes.

That's a scary list to find gossip in, isn't it?

Here are three key questions to ask yourself if you want to avoid being a gossip:

1. **Is this my information to share?**
2. **Would I be comfortable being identified as the source of this information?**

3. Does this really need to be said or do I just really need something to say?

By the way, there's a special subset of gossip that gets addressed in the Bible called mockery. I consider it a subset of gossip because it involves taking something that is actually true about what someone does, says or believes and twisting it in a way that's derisive, dismissive, and destructive.

Mockers pay no attention to the strength of what someone says or believes. They aren't interested in a debate, because they're not interested in truth. Mockers are out to tear others down by making fun of what they believe. Mockers simply ridicule, often because they have no reasonable evidence to offer.

Of all the kinds of speech the Bible warns us about, mockery may be the most frustrating because those who employ it cannot be reasoned with. They aren't interested in reason, they are interested only in ridicule.

This might be why the Bible says:

> **Whoever corrects a mocker invites insults; whoever rebukes the wicked incurs abuse.**
>
> *- Proverbs 9:7*

The Bible actually implies that it's a total waste of time to try and engage with a mocker:

> **Do not rebuke mockers or they will hate you; rebuke the wise and they will love you.**
>
> *- Proverbs 9:8*

Because mockery does not seek to offer a reasoned argument against its enemies, it can often be associated with specific logical fallacies.

For example, often, mockery depends on taking something out of context so that it appears not only unreasonable but ridiculous or even evil. This is called the *contextomy fallacy.* For example, a medical study finds that, under certain very limited conditions, a drug has a statistically significant correlation with miscarriage and advocates of naturalistic medicine say "Big Pharma is out to kill babies!"

Other times, mockery takes something that was said to an absurd conclusion. This is called the *reductio ad absurdum fallacy*. For example, say a manager tells his CEO, "I think we should consider allowing a little more flexibility in work hours" to which the CEO responds, "That's stupid. If we do that, pretty soon no one will be showing up to work and we'll be bankrupt."

Mockery also occurs when the substance of a logical argument is ignored in favor of attacking the character, credentials, or competence of the person advancing it. This is called the *ad hominem fallacy*. For example, a Republican candidate might say "Why would you even consider the Democrat economic policies when they're allowing illegal immigration to destroy our society?" Or a Democrat candidate might say, "Why would you even consider the Republican economic policies when they're clearly anti-woman, given their stance on abortion?"

Slander

Slander is untrue and unkind.

Of course, those who engage in slander rarely admit either.

The Bible says this about slander:

> **Whoever conceals hatred with lying lips and spreads slander is a fool.**
>
> *- Proverbs 10:18*

Notice the part about "concealing hatred". Ultimately, slander comes from a heart that hopes to hurt someone. There is hatred boiling under the surface, but it is concealed by making up untruths or spreading untruths that someone else made up.

Slander doesn't say "I hate this person," slander says, "I can't believe this person did such and such!"

As with gossip, slander is deeply rooted in a general lack of concern about other human beings. And like gossip, it shows up in some pretty bad company in the Bible:

But now I am writing to you that you must not associate with anyone who claims to be a brother or sister but is sexually immoral or greedy, an idolater or slanderer, a drunkard or swindler. Do not even eat with such people.

- 1 Corinthians 5:11

For I am afraid that when I come I may not find you as I want you to be, and you may not find me as you want me to be. I fear that there may be discord, jealousy, fits of rage, selfish ambition, slander, gossip, arrogance and disorder.

- 2 Corinthians 12:20

Clearly, slander is something that every follower of Jesus has to steer clear of. And with that in mind, it's important to remember that we don't have to know that something is false to be guilty of slander.

Slander is spreading misinformation in order to hurt someone's reputation.

We can easily speak slander simply by not making any effort to verify what we share before we share it. As a general rule, if you want to honor God with your words, investigate before you propagate! There are whole websites, like Snopes.com that are devoted to investigating the truth of various claims that are circulating.

Slander also happens when we knowingly use truth to lead someone to a false conclusion. In other words, it's not that what we say is an outright lie, it's just not the whole truth. And that missing bit of truth is enough to lead the listener to a completely false conclusion.

There's an old story about the first mate on a merchant ship who got drunk one night. It was the only time it had ever happened during his several years onboard that ship and he went to the captain and apologized swearing it would never happen again.

The captain asked if it had ever happened before and the first mate hung his head and admitted that, yes, one time almost ten years ago he had gotten drunk.

The captain, who was jealous of how fast this man had been rising in the company ranks, wrote in the ship's logbook: "first mate was drunk again last night".

The first mate begged him to take it out because it would probably mean his job and would certainly mean that he wouldn't get promoted anymore. But the captain refused to remove it, defending himself by saying that what he had written was 100% true.

So the next day the first-mate recorded in the ship's logbook, "Praise God! The captain was sober last night!"

Both men spoke only truth, but both men still slandered.

Grace

If what we say is both true and kind, it is what the bible calls grace.

As we have already seen, grace is always kind...not in a nice, sanitized, polite way that is ultimately self-serving...but in a self-sacrificing way that may very well require as much or more of the speaker than of the one spoken to.

And of course, grace is also true. It is always true because, as we have already seen, there can be no true grace without truth. Grace begins with the truth and cannot exist without it.

But of course, grace does not use the truth to break but to build, to refine, to advance, to help, to heal.

Combining truth with kindness is not easy. It's tricky. But that's also what makes it so tasty.

9 - In These Last Days

In the first chapter of the book of Romans, the Apostle Paul describes a gradual descent into depravity. It began, he says, with a denial of God:

> **The wrath of God is being revealed from heaven against all the godlessness and wickedness of people, who suppress the truth by their wickedness, since what may be known about God is plain to them, because God has made it plain to them.**
>
> **For since the creation of the world God's invisible qualities-- his eternal power and**

> **divine nature-- have been clearly seen, being understood from what has been made, so that people are without excuse. For although they knew God, they neither glorified him as God nor gave thanks to him, but their thinking became futile and their foolish hearts were darkened.**

- Romans 1:18-21

As the descent into depravity continues, Paul speaks of sexual perversions:

> **Therefore God gave them over in the sinful desires of their hearts to sexual impurity for the degrading of their bodies with one another.**

- Romans 1:24

Growing up in the church, I often heard this taught in such a way that I came away with the impression that sexual immorality was the nadir of the decline.

However, this is not what Romans 1 says at all.

I do not deny that sexual immorality – and Romans 1 speaks of both heterosexual and homosexual immorality – is a stage in the decline into depravity. But anyone who reads on to the end of what Paul says here must conclude that sexual immorality in society is not the lowest point, it is only a stop along the way to the real bottom.

The lowest point, Paul says, is the way we treat one another and, specifically, the way we talk to and about one another. We have already looked at part of this passage, but it bears revisiting with this specific context in mind:

> **They have become filled with every kind of wickedness, evil, greed and depravity. They are full of envy, murder, strife, deceit and malice. They are gossips, slanderers, God-haters, insolent, arrogant and boastful; they invent ways of doing evil; they disobey their parents; they have no understanding, no fidelity, no love, no mercy. Although they know God's righteous decree that those who do such things deserve death, they not only continue to do these very things but also approve of those who practice them.**

- Romans 1:29-32

As a pastor, I am constantly asked the question: are we living in the end times?

I think we are, but not because of earthquakes or the glorification of sexual immorality.

I think we're living in the end times because of the justification of gossip and the glorification of slander, the normalization of insolent, arrogant and boastful speech...not only by those who reject Jesus but by those who claim to follow him.

Similarly, Paul warned the church at Colossae:

> **Because of these, the wrath of God is coming. You used to walk in these ways, in the life you once lived. But now you must also rid yourselves of all such things as these: anger, rage, malice, slander, and filthy language from your lips. Do not lie to each other, since you have taken off your old self with its practices and have put on the new self, which is being renewed in knowledge in the image of its Creator.**

- Colossians 3:6-10

And to his protégé in the pastorate, Timothy, Paul wrote:

> **But mark this: There will be terrible times in the last days. People will be lovers of themselves, lovers of money, boastful, proud, abusive, disobedient to their parents, ungrateful, unholy, without love, unforgiving, slanderous, without self-control, brutal, not lovers of the good, treacherous, rash, conceited, lovers of pleasure rather than lovers of God-- having a form of godliness but denying its power. Have nothing to do with such people.**

- 2 Timothy 3:1-5

Each time I read these passages - and there are even more of them in the Bible than we have considered here - I am struck by how much attention God is paying to our words and by the fact that the way we use our words is a sign of the end times.

When I look at the way we're talking to and about each other these days, I do think we might be getting close to the end!

It's not simply that gossip and slander are rampant in our culture today, they are almost foundational. It's almost like we don't know how to engage in any kind of serious discourse without resorting to such language.

Recently, I took a call from someone promoting a political candidate running for state office here in Colorado. She asked if I had a minute for her to tell me about why I should vote for this particular candidate. Usually, I would say "no" and hang up, but for some reason, I said I had a few minutes and would be happy to listen.

Immediately the woman started into what was obviously a reading of a script. In about 15 seconds she had given me some basic background information on her candidate and then proceeded into a diatribe against her candidate's opponent.

I interrupted her and said, very politely, "I'm not interested in hearing about how awful the opposition is. I'm only interested in what your candidate's policies and plans are."

"Oh," she said, "...sure...I understand..."

There was a long pause as she was presumably looking over the script.

"Ok," she finally continued, "...oh...no..."

More silence.

"Well, she...no...you didn't want to hear anything negative so I can't say that..."

More silence.

Finally: "Um, well...did you have any questions for me?"

She literally couldn't find anything else in her script that wasn't just an attack on the opposition.

Look, attacking your opponent has long been a staple of politics, but today it seems to be the only thing anyone knows how to do!

When we look at what the Bible says and find that many will stand before God condemned on the basis of their gossip, slander and filthy language as much as on their sexual immorality and their idolatry...how can we read those words and not be deeply concerned about our own words?

Conversely, our words are not only the source of condemnation, but of affirmation. It is the way we use our words that identifies us as followers as God's people:

As we have seen, Jesus identified our words as one of the clearest indicators of the status of our relationship with him:

For the mouth speaks what the heart is full of. A good man brings good things out of the good stored up in him, and an evil man brings evil things out of the evil stored up in him. But I tell you that everyone will have to give account on the day of judgment for every empty word they have spoken. For by your words you will be acquitted, and by your words you will be condemned.

- Matthew 12:34b-37

Likewise King David asked and answered a critical question about those who would claim to be part of God's household:

LORD, who may dwell in your sacred tent? Who may live on your holy mountain? The one whose walk is blameless, who does what is righteous, who speaks the truth from their heart; whose tongue utters no slander, who does no wrong to a neighbor, and casts no slur on others;

- Psalm 15:1-3

10- Which Spirit Is Speaking?

Before we wrap up this conversation, I think it might be helpful to return again to the words of James. We've already looked at what James says about the tongue being like the bit in a horse's mouth or the rudder of a ship, in the sense that, though being a small part, it has a disproportionate power to affect the whole. But there is a context James gives to that analogy we haven't yet considered:

Not many of you should become teachers, my fellow believers, because you know that we who teach will be judged more strictly.

- James 3:1

Most people think of this verse as being applicable only to preachers, but I think that's a mistake. The truth is, every time we open our mouths or fire off a text or post a comment, we're teaching.

We're teaching people what we think and believe. We're teaching them what we think *they* should think and believe. We're teaching them what we think about them and about others. And of course, ultimately, whether we're conscious of it or not, we're teaching them what we think and believe about God.

What James says here is more than just a warning about pursuing an office or a position in the church. It's a warning about opening our mouths and casting our words into the world without thinking about what those words will teach others about us and the God we claim to represent.

I think this is why James goes on, after this initial warning, to say:

> **We all stumble in many ways. Anyone who is never at fault in what they say is perfect, able to keep their whole body in check.**
>
> *- James 3:2*

I think what James is saying is that not many people should look to become *explicit* teachers because we're all *implicit* teachers, whether we realize it or not, and, unfortunately, none of us have a great track record as teachers.

We all stumble in many ways.

Actually, there's an interesting translation issue here.

Most English versions of the Bible have something along those lines, saying that we stumble in many "ways" (NIV, NAS, ESV) or give offense in many "things" (KJV). But in the original Greek of this verse, there's no word for "ways" or "things". A more literal translation would be: *for we all stumble much*.

I think that's interesting. The addition of words like "ways" or "much" makes it sound like James is saying "we all sin in a variety of ways."

And of course, that's true. We do all sin in many ways.

But I don't think that's what James is saying. He's not reminding us of the variety of ways we miss the mark, cross the line, or twist what's right and good into something very different.

I think James is still laser-focused here on our words. I think he's saying that we all stumble much when it comes to what our words teach others.

That's why he goes on to say that anyone who is never at fault in what they say is *perfect*...because the tongue is the hardest part of the body to bring into submission to God. It's the last part of our sinful selves that surrenders.

I think this is why Jesus said:

> **"You have heard that it was said to the people long ago, 'You shall not murder, and anyone who murders will be subject to judgment.' But I tell you that anyone who is angry with a brother or sister will be subject to judgment. Again, anyone who says to a brother or sister, 'Raca,' is answerable to the court. And anyone who says, 'You fool!' will be in danger of the fire of hell.**
>
> *- Matthew 5:21-22*

Anyone who *says* "Raca". Anyone who *says* "You fool!"

Why this emphasis on what we *say*?

It's not that what we do doesn't matter or that what we say matters *more* than what we do. It's just that it's so easy to pat ourselves on the back because of what we haven't done when what we have said is just as important.

And what we *say* is often harder to get a handle on.

The reality is that, when we come to Jesus, we often find that it's easier to bring our hands under control than our tongues. It's easier to stop committing violence with physical weapons than with our words.

We all stumble much when it comes to our words.

I've never hit my wife.

I've never physically abused my children.

But I've spoken words that hit harder than any fist. I've said things that were sharper than any blade.

How about you?

It's in the context of this reality and this realization that James goes on to say what we've already considered:

> **When we put bits into the mouths of horses to make them obey us, we can turn the whole animal. Or take ships as an example. Although they are so large and are driven by strong winds, they are steered by a very small rudder wherever the pilot wants to go. Likewise, the tongue is a small part of the body, but it makes great boasts.**
>
> *- James 3:3-5a*

By the way, there's another interesting translation issue here. The Greek word that's translated here as "boasts" is an unusual one. It's not the normal word for "boasts". It's not even the word that James usually uses.

I think "boasts" is the right way to translate this word, but I think the reason James chose this particular word is that he wasn't talking about "bragging." I think James was talking about the legitimate great power of the tongue.

We use the English word "boast" in the same way sometimes:

This new technology boasts the power to revolutionize our industry.

Our country boasts some of the most breathtaking scenery in the world.

Our starting lineup boasts some of the best talent in the NFL.

His point is just that, like a small bit in the mouth of a big horse or a small rudder on a big boat, the tongue is small, but it has a disproportionate amount of power: the tongue boasts the ability to do big things.

Nothing really new there. We've already seen how powerful our words are.

But there's another part of this analogy that doesn't usually get much of our attention. We tend to focus here on the idea that a little thing can have such a big impact, but that focus can make us miss something else James is saying.

Think about this: The bit in the horse's mouth is controlled by the rider. The rudder is controlled by the pilot.

Both the bit and the rider are small things with disproportionate power...but they're also things that are under someone's control.

So if the tongue is like the bit and the rudder in that it's a small thing with a disproportionate amount of power...is it also like them in that it's under the control of someone?

Of course it is.

So here's the big question: **who has control of your tongue?**

To some extent, the answer is: *we* do.

We have control of our tongues...at least to a degree.

All of the proverbs and other biblical instruction we've looked at in this book assume that we have at least *some* control over our own tongues.

There's no point in urging us to be "slow to speak" if we can't choose when we speak and when we don't. There's no point in telling us to let our conversations "be always full of grace" if we have no control over the content.

But are we the *only* ones with control of our tongues?

I don't think so.

There are two interesting incidents in the Gospels which suggest we are not the only ones who have control of our tongues.

At a pivotal point in his ministry, Jesus began to tell his disciples about the plan for him to suffer and die before being raised back to life.

Peter - who I can't help but wonder if James was thinking of when he said we need to be "slow to speak"! – didn't love that plan. So:

> **Peter took him aside and began to rebuke him. "Never, Lord!" he said. "This shall never happen to you!"**
>
> **Jesus turned and said to Peter, "Get behind me, Satan! You are a stumbling block to me; you do not have in mind the concerns of God, but merely human concerns."**

- Matthew 16:22-23

Now, I don't think Jesus meant this literally. I don't think he was saying Peter was possessed by the devil.

By the way, many Christians are surprised to learn that the Bible never talks about demonic "possession". While some English translations do use language about people being "possessed by a demon"[6] the underlying Greek is more literally translated as "in an unclean spirit" or "had a demon" or, often, "demonized." In other words, the original Greek speaks not so much of ownership or absolute possession but rather of the ongoing presence and influence of such spirits in the lives of human beings.

---

[6] For instance, the NIV uses this phrase in Mark 1:23, 3:22, 5:15, 7:25, 9:17; Luke 4:33; John 8:49, 10:21.

And clearly Jesus is saying here that Peter was not immune to such influence.

I don't think Jesus wasn't saying that Peter needed an exorcism, or else he would have performed one. I think, instead, Jesus was clueing us in to an important reality: **our spirit isn't the only spirit with access to our tongues.**

Now the idea that Satan and his forces have some ability to influence what and how we speak is probably a little alarming, but here's the good news: **God's Spirit also has the ability to influence what and how we speak.**

When Jesus warned his disciples that they would be persecuted for their faith in him, he also told them:

> **But when they arrest you, do not worry about what to say or how to say it. At that time you will be given what to say, for it will not be you speaking, but the Spirit of your Father speaking through you.**

Matthew 10:19-20

As with Peter and Satan, I'm not sure Jesus meant this literally, at least not in every case, though I do believe the Holy Spirit may at times take over someone's tongue. I'm just saying that, in most cases, the owner of the tongue has to make a choice about who he or she grants access to that tongue.[7]

Does this mean that we aren't responsible for what we say? That it's just Satan or the Holy Spirit?

No.

Obviously, it's not *always* Satan or the Holy Spirit, but I think, even when those spirits are involved, it's still pretty rare that we don't have at least some responsibility for our words.

We are almost always responsible for our words, but part of that responsibility involves the obligation to choose which spirits we allow access to our tongues (and, of course, nowadays, our fingers).

I have discovered that one advantage of being "slow to speak" is that it allows me time to ask myself a very important question: *what spirit is trying to speak through me in this moment?*

And it's not just the question of whether it's Satan or the Holy Spirit. I also have to ask myself if the spirit of fear is trying to speak, or if the spirit of pride is trying to speak, or

---

[7] For more on this, see 1 Corinthians 14:29-32 where Paul urges prophets – i.e. those through whom the Holy Spirit manifests himself in prophetic utterances – to speak in an orderly fashion because, "the spirits of prophets are subject to the control of prophets." Even though it is the Holy Spirit manifesting himself, there is a degree to which human beings have a say in how/when the prophecies are delivered.

if the spirit of insecurity is trying to speak, or if the spirit of control is trying to speak. Ultimately, these are all spirits under our enemy, who the Bible calls the "spirit of the world":

What we have received is not the spirit of the world, but the Spirit who is from God, so that we may understand what God has freely given us.

This is what we speak, not in words taught us by human wisdom but in words taught by the Spirit, explaining spiritual realities with Spirit-taught words.

- 1 Corinthians 2:12-13

We see here, again, the contrast between these two fundamentally different spirits that seek, perhaps even long (though from radically different motivations), to speak through us.

But again, it's ultimately up to us which spirits we give access to our tongues.

This might all sound very spiritual and mystical, and to some extent it is. When I remember to be "slow to speak" and therefore have the space to discern which spirit is motivating the words I want to speak into the world, and when I invite the Holy Spirit to speak through me, something powerful happens. In those moments, I find that I am able to speak words that are not only more helpful, but more helpful than I am actually capable of being. In those moments, I often find myself saying things and then immediately thinking "where did that come from?"

But, while there is a somewhat mystical facet to all this, there's also a very practical one: we don't grant different spirits access to our tongues only in the moment we are shaping our words, but in the thousand moments before it that shaped us.

In other words, we grant different spirits access to our tongues long before we start to speak.

The spirit to which we grant access to our tongues is often determined by the spirit to which we have given access to our minds.

What I mean is that what comes *out* of us is often determined by what we've allowed to go *into* us.

If we are granting the spirit of this world too much access to our minds by what we listen to or watch, we shouldn't be surprised to hear the words of that spirit coming out of us.

If we listen to movies with a lot of cussing, what kinds of words are likely to come out of us the next time we step on one of the kids' Legos?

If we listen to a lot of crude jokes, what kinds of jokes are we likely to tell at the office Christmas party?

If we listen to a lot of angry music, what emotion is likely to shape our conversations with others?

Now, some people will push back on what I'm saying here as being too legalistic. And some will even quote Jesus who said:

> **"What goes into someone's mouth does not defile them, but what comes out of their mouth, that is what defiles them."**
>
> *- Matthew 15:11*

There is a general principle here about righteousness. The principle is that what we push out into the world is more significant than what we take in from it.

But there are two things we need to keep in mind.

First, when Jesus talked about what goes into someone's mouth, he was speaking literally, not figuratively. He wasn't talking about which spirits we're giving access to our hearts and minds by what we take in. He was talking about the literal foods we eat with our mouths, addressing the Judaic concept of clean and unclean foods. His point was that eating an "unclean" food doesn't determine whether or not we are morally righteous. It's a mistake to generalize too much about what we watch and listen to based on this instruction which is really focused on physical food.

Second, while it is true that, metaphorically speaking, what we *send out* is more important than what we *take in* when it comes to being righteous, this does not mean that what we take in doesn't impact what we send out.

The Bible is very clear that what we take in matters.

> **My son, pay attention to what I say; turn your ear to my words. Do not let them out of your sight, keep them within your heart; for they are life to those who find them and health to one's whole body. Above all else, guard your heart, for everything you do flows from it.**

- Proverbs 4:20-23

Notice that the admonition to "guard your heart" is closely linked to what we "pay attention" to. Notice also that what we do flows from what has been allowed into our hearts by virtue of what we have paid attention to.

Like it or not, when enough of something has been poured into us, it's going to start leak out.

It's probably also worth pointing out that the very next verse after this instruction to guard our hearts is:

> **Keep your mouth free of perversity; keep corrupt talk far from your lips.**

- Proverbs 4:23

The context makes it clear that keeping our mouths free of perversity is closely connected to guarding our hearts by being careful about what goes into them.

The Apostle Paul also warned us about the power of what we're paying attention to (i.e. taking in) and pondering:

> **Finally, brothers and sisters, whatever is true, whatever is noble, whatever is right, whatever is pure, whatever is lovely, whatever is admirable-- if anything is excellent or praiseworthy-- <u>think about such things</u>.**
>
> *- Philippians 4:8*

If we fail to pay attention to such commands, and in this failure find ourselves giving the spirit of the world too much access to our hearts and minds, we might find that our tongues are tools of a spirit we didn't even know had taken control.

11 - The Final Word

You know what's nice about the fact that words are so powerful?

You don't need a lot of words to do a lot of good.

Think about how many incredible, life-changing moments happen with just a few words.

Yes.

I do.

You passed.

You qualified.

I'm proud of you.

It's a boy.

It's a girl.

You're hired.

You're promoted.

You're in remission.

I'm sorry.

I was wrong.

Forgive me.

I forgive you.

I love you.

Welcome home.

What makes words so dangerous is also the very thing that makes them such an incredible tool for good.

I titled this book, and began it, with that familiar phrase "sticks and stones".

I chose that title for three different reasons.

First, it's a familiar phrase that I hoped would, in a somewhat light-hearted way, clue you in to the subject of this book: words.

Second, it's a ridiculous saying and we all know it. The idea that sticks and stones can break our bones but words will never hurt us...that's not just inaccurate, it's *insidious*. It gives some a false justification for using words lightly when in fact, they carry tremendous weight.

Maybe worse, it leaves others feeling weak and ashamed when we can't seem to recover from someone's words.

What's wrong with me? Why did what she say affect me so much? Why can't I get what he said out of my head? They're only words!

But there's really no "only" about them, is there?

As we discussed, the wounds caused by words often heal much more slowly – if at all – than those caused by actual sticks and stones.

So by calling the book *Sticks and Stones*, I was getting a head start on one of its most important premises: words are powerful.

Third, and this is the most important reason I went with *Sticks and Stones*: words, just like sticks and stones, can be put to radically different purposes.

The old adage about sticks and stones only builds upon one of their potential uses: harm.

But the sticks and stones that can break can also be used to build.

I got whacked by a lot of sticks growing up, playing pirates and running through the woods...but I also built a lot of cool forts with sticks. Treehouses too. I didn't enjoy it as much as building forts, but I also helped my grandparents string chicken wire between sticks we drove into the ground to protect their garden from deer.

When I was in high school, I started pole vaulting. I was pretty good, but not great. I could vault about 13 feet, which is nothing compared to the world record (now at 20'6"), but honestly, it wasn't even very close to what some other guys my age were doing back them.

But here's the thing: I couldn't go crazy high with that stick, but it got me WAY higher than I could have gone without it. The world's record high jump is 8'.46" which is hard to imagine…but I was clearing more than that the first month I joined the track team as a freshman. I just needed a stick to do it!

I got more than a few welts from stones growing up, too, playing…well, I don't actually remember what we were playing but we threw a lot of rocks at each other! But I also created a lot of really cool pools by building dams with stones.

Coletta and I recently hiked the West Highland Way in Scottland. The trail was well-worn, so for the most part there was no need to mark it. There was one section, however, called the Devil's Staircase where we saw piles or rocks (called cairns) every few feet. They were there because, when the snow starts to fall in the highlands and the trail gets covered, you'd be lost in a matter of minutes without them.

And just so you know, I'm still playing with sticks and stones.

I spend a lot of what little spare time I have in my shop creating interesting things with wood. And sometimes the wood is actually sticks. I love putting sticks in a plastic container, filling the voids between them with epoxy resin, sticking the whole thing on a lathe and carving out a unique vase or bowl.

And I love a good rock! Fortunately, I married an earth sciences teacher whose dad also taught geology, so in addition to an incredible partner, I got a lot of cool rocks when I married Coletta.

And if you come to my house, at the corner of the back yard is a big rock with a bunch of smaller rocks piled on top of it. The big rock was there when we bought the house, but we put the other ones on top of it. They're our standing stones.

We've put them there at significant points in our life, to commemorate God's faithfulness to us thus far and remind us that we can trust Him going forward. Each of our girls added a stone when they went off to college. Every time I see them I'm reminded of the Foundation on which our lives are built.

Yes, sticks and stones can break, but they can also build.

The same sticks that can be used to poke and prod, to bash and bruise, to break...can also be used to support what has been broken while it heals, to keep a prowling enemy at bay while we wait for dawn, to build a wall to protect what needs protecting.

The same sticks that can be used to pen us in a prison from which we feel we'll never escape...can also be used to set us free, a way to vault over a barrier too high to ever leap.

The same stones that can leave us stunned and stumbling, concussed and confused about the way forward...can also be used to mark the way through the wilderness, cairns that tell us we're on the right path when the light is growing dim and the snow is getting deep.

The same stones that can be used to strike and sting...can also be used to make staircases by which we leave dark caverns behind and ascend into the light.

Sticks and stones may break our bones...but they can also bind them up and give us something solid to stand on.

That's the dual potential of our words.

My hope is that my words about words will help you use your words to do far more building than breaking.

I leave you with these words. We've considered them already, but I can think of no more fitting benediction for this book or antidote to the danger we face every time we open our mouths (or wiggle our fingers):

Gracious words are a honeycomb, sweet to the soul and healing to the bones.

- Proverbs 16:24

About the Author

Craig A. Smith is the lead pastor of Mission Hills Church, a multi-campus church located in the Front Range of Colorado. He and his wife, Coletta, have two adult daughters, Rochelle and Lynae.

Craig holds an M.Div. from Denver Seminary and a Ph.D. in Biblical Studies from Trinity College, Bristol University in the U.K.

He is the author of several books including *How (Not) To Miss God Moving, The Kingdom for the Kingless, The Search, The Voice, The Word: Understanding and Trusting the Bible in an Age of Skepticism*, as well as several academic articles and a dissertation on identifying literary structures in biblical material.

Craig's greatest passion is helping people dig deep into God's Word and reach wide into the world for God's glory and for the good of those we serve as followers of Jesus.

For more information about Craig, visit his website:

www.craigasmith.org

Made in the USA
Monee, IL
02 October 2024